THE OFFICIAL ACTIVITY BOOK OF THE

PALDEA REGION

PIKACHU PRESS ™

Pokémon - The Official Activity Book of the Paldea Region
$12.99 USA
$17.99 CAN

The Pokémon Company
INTERNATIONAL

Publisher: Heather Dalgleish
Sr. Publishing Manager: Mark Hughes
Art Director: Chris Franc
Design Manager: Hiromi Kimura
Designer: Lauren Parra
Director, Editing: Anja Weinbach
Editors: Eoin Sanders, Stephen "Phen" Crane, and Laura Temple
Director, Brand Services: Amy Ganster
Brand Services Manager: Wendy Hoover
Brand Services Partner: Doug Walsh
Page Layout Designer: Erin Fahringer
Writer: Sonia Sander

The Pokémon Company International
10400 NE 4th Street, Suite 2800
Bellevue, WA 98004 USA

3rd Floor Building 10, Chiswick Park,
566 Chiswick High Road
London, W4 5XS United Kingdom

The Pokémon Company International Ireland Limited
3rd Floor, 2 Central Plaza, Dame Street
Dublin 2, D02 T0X4, Ireland

Retain these addresses for your records.

Visit us on the web at www.pokemon.com

Printed in Hui Zhou, Guangdong, China by 1010 Printing International Ltd.
This book was produced by Quarto Publishing Group USA Inc.

First printing October 2023.

23 24 25 26 27 5 4 3 2 1

ISBN: 978-1-60438-245-7

THE OFFICIAL ACTIVITY BOOK OF THE

PALDEA REGION

WELCOME TO THE PALDEA REGION

The three Paldea first partner friends—Sprigatito, Fuecoco, and Quaxly—as well as your old friend Pikachu are here to travel with you through this brand-new activity book that's chock full of activities. Are you ready to meet the newly discovered Paldea Pokémon? Then, let's get started!

PALDEA REGION POKÉMON HEIGHT & WEIGHT CHART

Here's a handy reference sheet for some of the tougher puzzles! Refer to this information when you're stuck, or if you want to brush up on some of the Pokémon living in the Paldea region that we've discovered so far. Only the Pokémon found in this activity book are listed in this chart.

MAKE YOUR OWN POKÉMON BOOKMARKS

Four origami bookmarks included in this book allow you to take Pikachu and the three Paldea first partner friends, Sprigatito, Fuecoco, and Quaxly, along with you on all of your reading adventures. You can even use one of the bookmarks to help you keep track of your progress in this activity book. But first, carefully cut out each template sheet needed. Then, follow the step-by-step folding instructions for each of the four Pokémon bookmarks. Now, you just need to decide which Pokémon will adorn your favorite Pokémon book!

WORD SEARCH WONDER

The three Paldea first partner Pokémon, Sprigatito, Fuecoco, and Quaxly are listed below with some of their Pokémon friends. Can you find and circle every one? You'll have to search across, down, and even diagonal!

ARMAROUGE
AXEW
AZURILL
CHEWTLE
DIGLETT
DRAGONITE
EEVEE
FIDOUGH
FLETCHLING
FUECOCO
GARCHOMP
GYARADOS
HERACROSS
HOPPIP
KORAIDON
LECHONK
LITLEO
MIMIKYU
MIRAIDON
PAWMI
PIKACHU
PSYDUCK
QUAXLY

RAICHU
ROTOM
SPRIGATITO
SWABLU
UMBREON
VAPOREON
WHISCASH

```
J L S L Q P U M B R E O N W Y Y Q
R E W F S F F L E T C H L I N G O
C C A R Y P P F I L I T L E O N Y
P H B V A M R N P C B A X E W M U
S O L A W I O I N K O R A I D O N
Y N U P P G C D G O P K E A P R A
D K Y O A J L H V A T W J R I G Z
U Z P R W Y G O U M T H I M K Y U
C T D E M V G E H I M I E A A A R
K F V O I K E G O R I S T R C R I
K Z I N C V U H P A M C Q O H A L
D I G L E T T A P I I A U U U D L
G C H E W T L E I D K S A G K O N
R O T O M U C I P O Y H X E F S I
F I D O U G H X V N U D L J V K W
K D I G A R C H O M P J Y T C D F
H E R A C R O S S E F U E C O C O
```

ANSWERS ON PAGE 89

CLUED IN CLOSE-UP

Do you have a nose for sleuthing? Are you detail-oriented? Then, you should have no problem finding and circling the matching close-up image to Lechonk's full image.

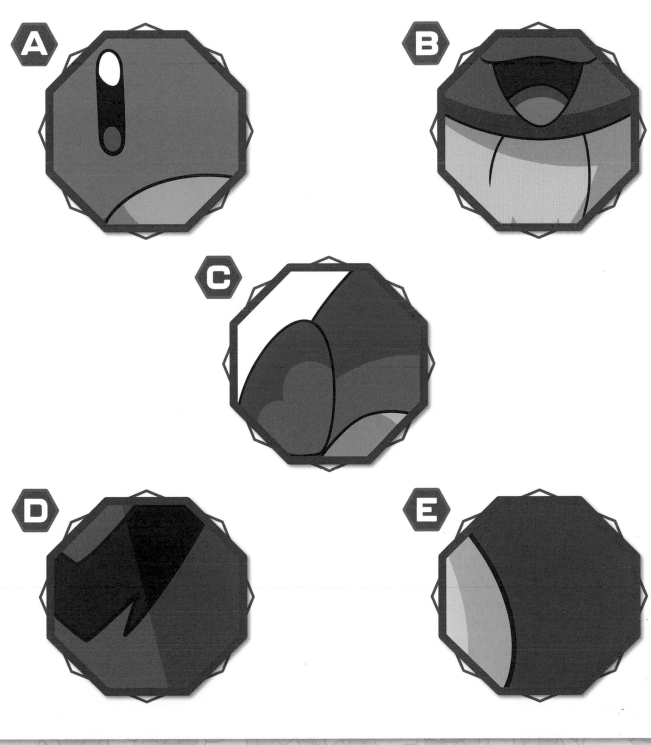

A

B

C

D

E

SCRAMBLING TO UNSCRAMBLE

How fast can you help Pikachu unscramble the names of five of its newly discovered friends from the Paldea region? Set your timer and begin unscrambling!

1 ELDUERCEG

_____

2 RIFFGAAIR

_____

3 WPMIA

_____

4 AYUXQL

_____

5 TGLITWE

_____

ANSWERS ON PAGE 89

POKÉ BALL PATTERN

Can you follow the Poké Ball pattern all the way through from the start to the finish? In order to succeed at this test, you must always follow the same four Poké Ball patterns exactly as shown below, over and over again as the pattern repeats, until you reach the end. Remember, you may only move horizontally and vertically.

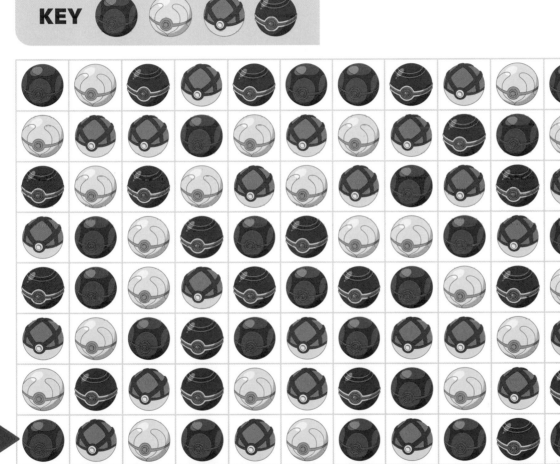

QUIZ QUEST

In this quest, you will be given four options to choose from. Choose wisely and move ahead, choose poorly and you'll have to start again. If you need a little help along the way, you can refer to the height and weight charts included in this book.

1 Which one of these Pokémon is NOT an Evolution of Eevee?

- ☐ A. Vaporeon
- ☐ B. Umbreon
- ☐ C. Lechonk
- ☐ D. Jolteon

2 Which one of these Pokémon is NOT an Electric type?

- ☐ A. Pawmi
- ☐ B. Dedenne
- ☐ C. Pikachu
- ☐ D. Smoliv

3 Which one of these Pokémon weighs less than 55 lbs?

- ☐ A. Grafaiai
- ☐ B. Great Tusk
- ☐ C. Sprigatito
- ☐ D. Miraidon

4 Which one of these Pokémon has a tail?

- ☐ A. Klawf
- ☐ B. Koraidon
- ☐ C. Bellibolt
- ☐ D. Ceruledge

ANSWERS ON PAGE 89

EYE ON EVOLUTION

Can you remember the order of Evolution or whether a Pokémon does or does not evolve? This true or false challenge will test that knowledge.

TRUE   FALSE

1. Lechonk evolves into Oinkologne.

2. Skeledirge is the final Evolution of Fuecoco.

3. Smoliv evolves into Dollic.

4. Sprigatito is the final Evolution of Floragato.

5. Tadbulb evolves into Bellibolt.

6. Bonsly doesn't evolve.

7. Fraxure's final Evolution is Axew.

8. Swablu evolves into Altaria.

9. Finneon doesn't evolve.

10. Barboach evolves into Whiscash.

ANSWERS ON PAGE 89

GUESS THE POKÉMON

If you were given a few clues, would you be able to figure out the Pokémon? The stats are provided below. But you need to fill in the Pokémon names. If you need a hint, take a look at the Pokémon featured on the page.

1
TYPE: Electric/Dragon
CATEGORY: Paradox
IT MUST BE:

2
TYPE: Ice
CATEGORY: Terra Whale
IT MUST BE:

3
TYPE: Fighting/Dragon
CATEGORY: Paradox
IT MUST BE:

4
TYPE: Fire
CATEGORY: Fire Croc
IT MUST BE:

5
TYPE: Fire/Ghost
CATEGORY: Fire Blades
IT MUST BE:

6
TYPE: Ground/Fighting
CATEGORY: Paradox
IT MUST BE:

ANSWERS ON PAGE 89

MIGHTY MAZE

Draw a line along the path that Pikachu needs to take in order to find its Electric-type Pokémon friend.

FINISH

FINISH

START

FINISH

STAND TALL AND MEASURE UP

It's a tall order to line up Pokémon correctly. Do you have the know-how to arrange them without any clues? Fear not, if you need a little help, you can always refer to the height and weight charts at the back of this book. Number these Pokémon from shortest to tallest from one to six.

QUAXLY

_____

WIGLETT

_____

FARIGIRAF

_____

FIDOUGH

_____

CYCLIZAR

_____

KLAWF

_____

ANSWERS ON PAGE 89

DUAL-TYPE MATCH-UP

In this task, you will be asked to test your knowledge of dual-type Pokémon. Even if you can spot them, can you be sure of both their types? Draw a line from the Pokémon name to its corresponding types.

GYARADOS

KROKOROK

LARVITAR

FIRE/PSYCHIC

FIRE/GHOST

NORMAL/FLYING

POISON/NORMAL

WATER/FLYING

GROUND/DARK

ROCK/GROUND

NORMAL/FLYING

CERULEDGE

SWABLU

GRAFAIAI

FLETCHLING

ARMAROUGE

ANSWERS ON PAGE 90

SUDOKU SKILL SET

To win this challenge, you must use four of the Pokémon type symbols—Fire, Water, Grass, and Electric—to fill the grid below. We have started you off with four squares already filled in. Now you must fill the remaining squares. But keep in mind that you can only use a symbol once in each column and row. You also cannot repeat the symbols within the smaller 4x4 squares that are marked out in the grid.

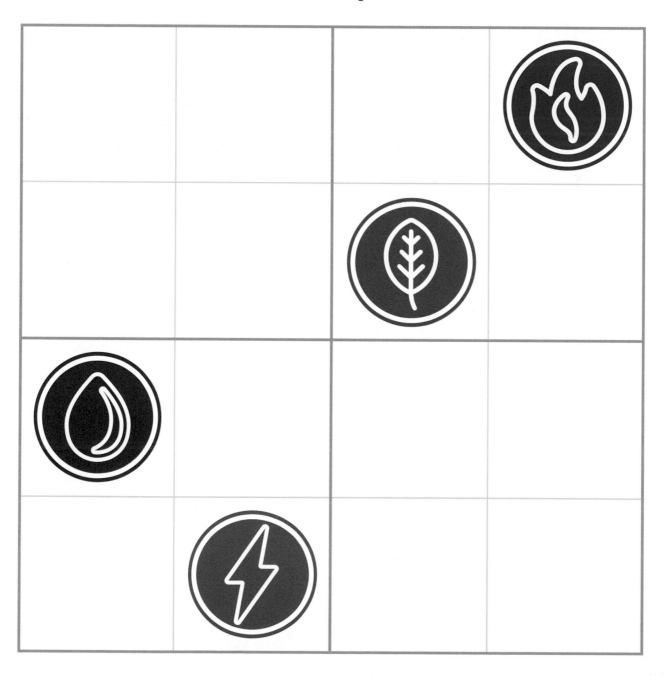

ANSWERS ON PAGE 90

DARE TO DECODE

You've proven your decoding skills with your first task. This time, set a timer to see how fast you can solve the missing words. Use the key provided to help break the code and solve the message.

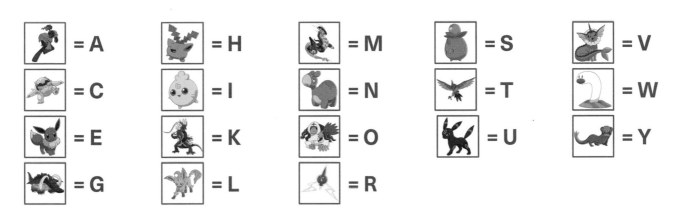

This _____ -type Pokémon,

_____ ,

_____ for food all day with its

_____ of

_____ .

PUZZLING OVER POKÉMON

Quaxly is missing a few key pieces to its puzzle. Each piece only fits in a specific spot. Can you draw a line from each missing piece to its proper home?

ANSWERS ON PAGE 90

PATH OF THE GRASS-TYPE POKÉMON

Sprigatito needs help making its way down a path through a maze of Pokémon. But it can only travel the path that Grass-type Pokémon have taken. Start at the top and lead Sprigatito down to the finish line.

START

FINISH

CROSSWORD CHALLENGE

Are you a crossword puzzle genius? Prove your ability using the Pokémon descriptions to identify all ten of the Pokémon featured in this crossword puzzle. If you need a hint, check out the Pokémon pictured around the puzzle.

ANSWERS ON PAGE 90

ACROSS

2. The extension and contraction of this Electric-type Pokémon's muscles generates electricity. It glows when in trouble.

3. This friendly Pokémon doesn't like being alone. Pay it even the slightest bit of attention, and it will follow you forever.

5. The gel secreted by this Water-type Pokémon's feathers repels water and grime.

7. This Plasma Pokémon's electricity-like body can enter some kinds of machines and take control in order to make mischief.

8. This Fire-type Pokémon lies on warm rocks and uses the heat absorbed by its square-shaped scales to create fire energy.

9. When this Electric-type Pokémon is angered, it immediately discharges the energy stored in the pouches in its cheeks.

DOWN

1. It was said this Fighting- and Dragon-type Pokémon split the land with its bare fists.

2. Its fluffy fur is similar in composition to plants. This Grass-type Pokémon frequently washes its face to keep it from drying out.

4. This Electric- and Dragon-type Pokémon resembles Cyclizar, but it is far more ruthless and powerful.

6. This Normal-type Pokémon possesses a keen sense of smell but doesn't use it for anything other than foraging.

WHO'S THAT POKÉMON?

Can you identify Pokémon just by their silhouette? This challenge will test that specific skill, as Sprigatito needs your help naming its Grass-type Pokémon friends.

1 _____

2 _____

3 _____

4 _____

5 _____

6 _____

ANSWERS ON PAGE 90

ARE YOU A QUAXLY EXPERT?

Are you an expert on Quaxly? Could you prove it? Here's your chance! Think carefully before you answer the questions below. Your ranking depends upon it.

1 Height: _____

2 Weight: _____

3 Type: _____

4 It is a _____ Pokémon.

5 Quaxly evolves into _____.

6 Quaxly wears a _____.

7 The gel secreted by its feathers repels _____ and _____.

8 Its weaknesses are _____ and _____.

- **1-2 answers correct:**
  You recognize who Quaxly is, but there's much more to learn.

- **3-4 answers correct:**
  You're just starting to get to know Quaxly.

- **5-6 answers correct:**
  It's clear to see that you're a big fan of Quaxly.

- **7-8 answers correct:**
  Congratulations! Without a doubt, you are a Quaxly expert!

ANSWERS ON PAGE 90

POKÉMON PATTERNS

This time, the pattern challenge features Pikachu and the three Paldea first partner Pokémon—Sprigatito, Fuecoco, and Quaxly. Remember, you must always follow the same Pokémon pattern exactly as shown below, over and over again as the pattern repeats, until you reach the end. Don't forget, you may only move horizontally and vertically.

KEY

FINISH

START

DARE TO DECODE

Sometimes, things are not as easy as they might look at first glance. In order to uncover the answer to this message, you must follow the correct twisted line to its corresponding empty space. Good luck!

NOT EVERY POKÉMON

NEWLY DISCOVERED PALDEA POKÉMON

Which of these are newly discovered Paldea Pokémon? Circle all the Pokémon first discovered in Paldea.

QUAXLY

SPRIGATITO

FUECOCO

LECHONK

PIKACHU

GRAFAIAI

PSYDUCK

CETITAN

ARMAROUGE

CYCLIZAR

BLISSEY

DIGLETT

ANSWERS ON PAGE 91

WORD SEARCH WONDER

Can you name all 18 different Pokémon types by heart? Double-check your memory with the complete list below. Then, find and circle every one in the puzzle. You'll have to search across, down, and even diagonally!

```
H T W L W F I G H T I N G Y N
B M A J F M M H W V A D T M O
W N U X B F T O O E D R M Y R
S Z C K R G Q S R N H A K P M
T D G U S O R T F S H G S O A
Y U U S H Q C A C M K O H B L
T I F T G T U K S C A N D W C
H L R I E A O B Q S B C I G H
A J E L E C T R I C I U U V P
M G B B V T T Q J Y C R G H O
L W R P S Y C H I C E Z V D I
Q K M T S C Q C S T C S S O S
P V E D A R K F A I R Y R V O
N W P F I R E W G R O U N D N
F L Y I N G S T E E L G I Q Q
```

BUG	FIRE	NORMAL
DARK	FLYING	POISON
DRAGON	GHOST	PSYCHIC
ELECTRIC	GRASS	ROCK
FAIRY	GROUND	STEEL
FIGHTING	ICE	WATER

ANSWERS ON PAGE 91

CLUED IN CLOSE-UP

How focused are you on the details? Can you match Quaxly's close-up image to its full image? Circle your final choice. Many eyes are watching to see how you do.

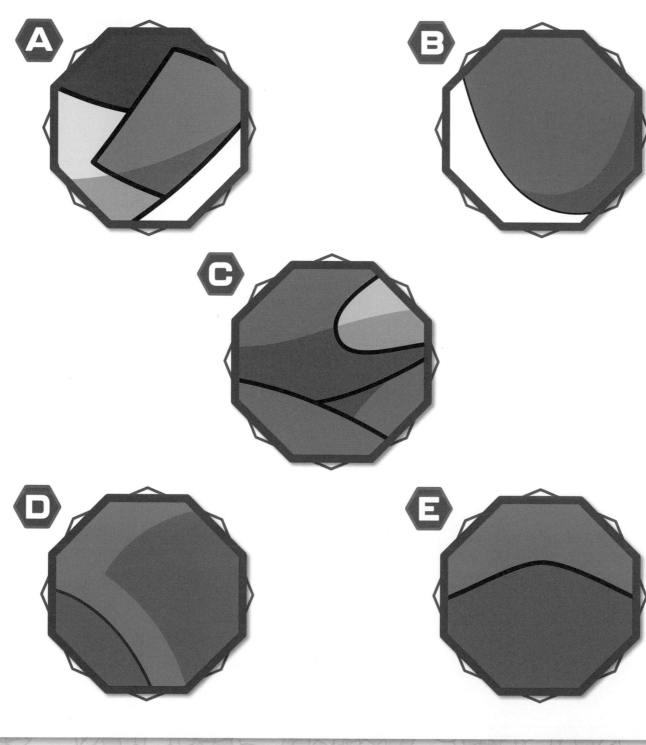

ANSWERS ON PAGE 91

QUIZ QUEST

Try to complete this quest on your own. The cleverest of Trainers will succeed without any aid. Don't forget, the height and weight charts are there if you need to refer to them.

1 Which one of these Pokémon is NOT a Water type?

- A. Psyduck
- B. Greavard
- C. Marill
- D. Quaxly

2 Which one of these dual-type Pokémon is a Flying type?

- A. Whiscash
- B. Great Tusk
- C. Cyclizar
- D. Gyarados

3 Which one of these Pokémon does NOT have a horn?

- A. Chewtle
- B. Heracross
- C. Axew
- D. Ceruledge

4 Which one of these Pokémon is taller than 12'?

- A. Cetitan
- B. Farigiraf
- C. Dragonite
- D. Armarouge

ANSWERS ON PAGE 91

TIME TO TIP THE SCALES

There is quite a range in weight between these Pokémon. Can you arrange them in order from lightest to heaviest? If you need a few hints, you can refer to the height and weight charts at the back of this book.

KLAWF

MIRAIDON

FUECOCO

PAWMI

CETITAN

GRAFAIAI

ANSWER:

1 _____

2 _____

3 _____

4 _____

5 _____

6 _____

ANSWERS ON PAGE 91

MIGHTY MAZE

Help lead Fuecoco toward the exit where another Fire-type Pokémon stands guard.

START

FINISH   FINISH   FINISH

ARE YOU A LECHONK EXPERT?

Are you an expert on Lechonk? Could you prove it? Here's your chance! Think carefully before you answer the questions below. Your ranking depends upon it.

1 Height: _____

2 Weight: _____

3 Type: _____

4 It is a _____ Pokémon.

5 Lechonk evolves into _____.

6 It has a keen _____.

7 Lechonk searches for _____.

8 Its nose is the color _____.

- **1-2 answers correct:**
  You recognize who Lechonk is, but there's much more to learn.

- **3-4 answers correct:**
  You're just starting to get to know Lechonk.

- **5-6 answers correct:**
  It's clear to see that you're a big fan of Lechonk.

- **7-8 answers correct:**
  Congratulations! Without a doubt, you're a Lechonk expert!

ANSWERS ON PAGE 91

POKÉMON PATTERNS

This round, you must follow a berry pattern all the way through from the start to the finish. In order to succeed at this tricky berry test, you must always follow the same four-berry pattern exactly as shown below, over and over again as the pattern repeats, until you reach the end. Remember, you may only move horizontally and vertically.

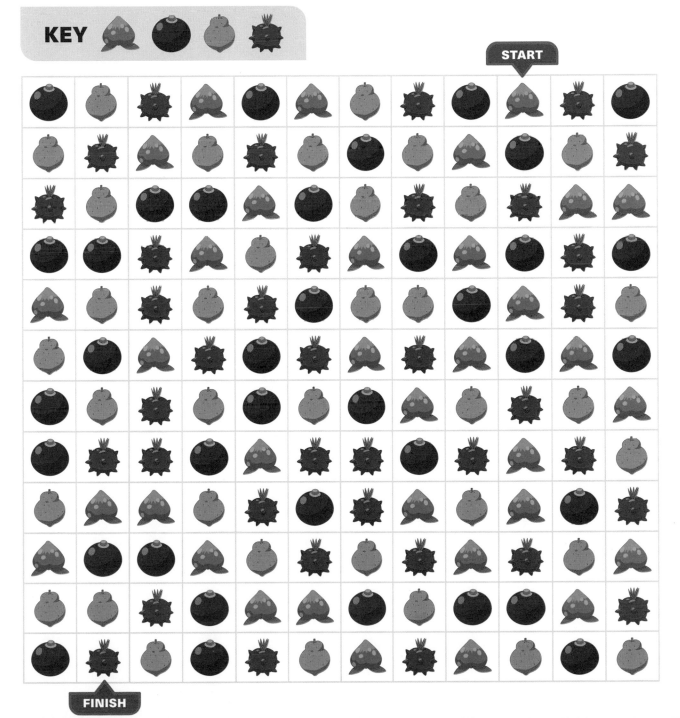

SCRAMBLING TO UNSCRAMBLE

You've tried your hand at this test before. Is there room for improvement? Help Pikachu unscramble the names of another five of its newly discovered friends from the Paldea region. This time, see if you can do it a little faster.

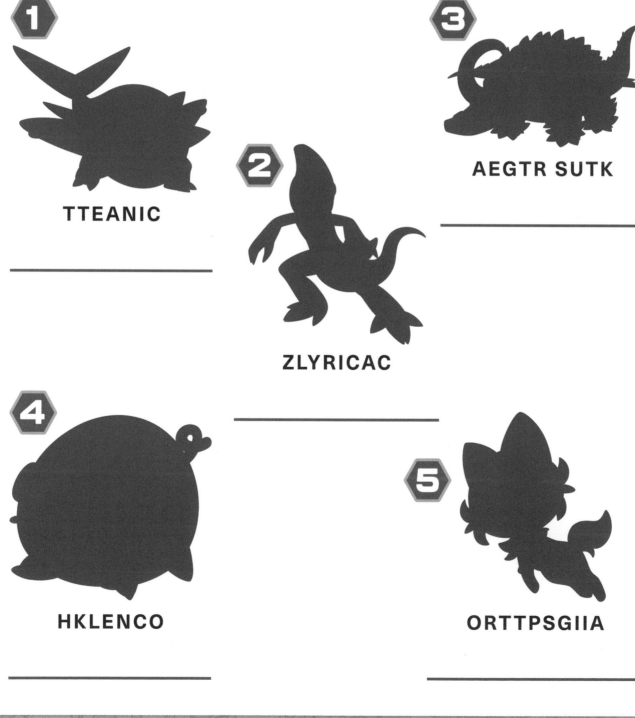

1
TTEANIC

_____

2
ZLYRICAC

_____

3
AEGTR SUTK

_____

4
HKLENCO

_____

5
ORTTPSGIIA

_____

ANSWERS ON PAGE 91

WHO'S THAT POKÉMON?

Ready for another round of identification checks? Look closely at these Pokémon silhouettes and then help Quaxly name its Water-type Pokémon friends.

PUZZLING OVER POKÉMON

This round, it's Sprigatito who is missing a few key pieces to its puzzle. Remember, each piece only fits in a specific spot. Can you draw a line from each missing piece to its proper home?

ANSWERS ON PAGE 92

PATH OF THE WATER-TYPE POKÉMON

Now, Quaxly needs help making its way down a path through a maze of Pokémon. But it can only travel the path that Water-type Pokémon have taken. Start at the top and lead Quaxly down to the finish line.

START

FINISH

HOW MANY CAN YOU NAME?

Test your knowledge of the newly discovered Paldea Pokémon featured in this book. If you get stuck, you can refer to the chart in the back of this book for a little help.

1 Only have one type: _____

_____

2 Do not evolve: _____

_____

3 Walk on all fours: _____

_____

4 Can fly: _____

5 Height is under 2': _____

_____

6 Are dual type: _____

_____

7 Weigh more than 100 lbs: _____

_____

8 Have tails: _____

_____

ANSWERS ON PAGE 92

EYE ON EVOLUTION

Get ready to test your Evolution know-how with another true or false challenge. You might be tempted to flip a coin to decide which answer to choose, but think twice about that strategy as it won't guarantee a perfect score.

		TRUE	FALSE
1	Armarouge and Ceruledge can both evolve into Charcadet.	☐	☐
2	Cyclizar evolves into Cetitan.	☐	☐
3	Girafarig evolves once into Farigiraf.	☐	☐
4	Dachsbun evolves into Fidough.	☐	☐
5	Houndstone is the final Evolution of Greavard.	☐	☐
6	Pawmo is the final Evolution of Pawmi.	☐	☐
7	Quaxly does not evolve.	☐	☐
8	Great Tusk does not evolve.	☐	☐
9	Miraidon and Koraidon do not evolve.	☐	☐
10	Pichu evolves into Pikachu.	☐	☐

ANSWERS ON PAGE 92

CROSSWORD CHALLENGE

It's time to test your crossword skill level again with ten more Pokémon descriptions. Don't forget that the Pokémon pictured are here for you in case you get stuck.

ANSWERS ON PAGE 92

DOWN

1. The color of the poisonous saliva depends on what the Toxic Monkey Pokémon eats. It covers its fingers in its saliva and draws patterns on trees in forests.

2. Its steel-hard head can shatter boulders. This Dragon-type Pokémon longingly hopes for wings to grow so it can fly.

4. It hangs upside-down from cliffs, waiting for prey. But it can't remain in this position for long because its blood rushes to its head.

5. This Fairy-type Pokémon is smooth and moist to the touch. Yeast in its breath induces fermentation in the Pokémon's vicinity.

7. The horns on its head provide a strong power that enables this Psychic- and Fairy-type Pokémon to sense people's emotions.

ACROSS

3. Sightings of this 705.5 lbs. Ground- and Fighting-type Pokémon have occurred in recent years. Its name was taken from a creature listed in a certain book.

6. Although its fur has many admirers, it is tough to raise as a pet because of its fickle meanness.

7. Its tail discharges electricity into the ground, protecting this Evolution of Pikachu from getting shocked.

8. It changes into the forms of others to surprise them. Apparently, it often transforms into a silent child.

9. This Garden Eel Pokémon can pick up the scent of a Veluza just over 65 feet away and will hide itself in the sand.

43

WORD SEARCH WONDER

By now, you should be able to recognize all 20 of the newly discovered Paldea Pokémon that are listed below. Can you find and circle every one? You'll have to search across, down and even diagonally!

ARMAROUGE
BELLIBOLT
CERULEDGE
CETITAN
CYCLIZAR
FARIGIRAF
FIDOUGH
FUECOCO
GRAFAIAI
GREAT TUSK
GREAVARD
KLAWF
KORAIDON
LECHONK
MIRAIDON
PAWMI
QUAXLY
SMOLIV
SPRIGATITO
WIGLETT

```
S P R I G A T I T O Y L H B X
G O Y P A W M I Q L W E Z E D
V G W A H O Q Q X I D C L L N
L R R R V M T A A R B H M L Q
P E G M M Y U L A P Z O V I V
D A R A L Q R V M R R N K B N
O T A R C I A P L E F K H O A
F T F O V E D R G A F N D L F
I U A U R T A D R T O I C T F
D S I G U Z E I T D A S E K U
O K A E I L G E I R B M T L E
U W I L U I L A O G I O I A C
G Q C R R G R K R P N L T W O
H Y E A I I Y T N J Q I A F C
C C F W M I A Y N O M V N I O
```

ANSWERS ON PAGE 92

ARE YOU A SPRIGATITO EXPERT?

Are you an expert on Sprigatito? Could you prove it? Here's your chance! Think carefully before you answer the questions below. Your ranking depends upon it.

1 Height: _____

2 Weight: _____

3 Type: _____

4 It is a _____ Pokémon.

5 Sprigatito evolves into _____.

6 It frequently _____ to keep it from drying out.

7 Sprigatito's eyes are the color _____.

8 Its fluffy fur is similar in composition to _____.

- **1-2 answers correct:**
  You recognize who Sprigatito is, but you have much to learn.
- **3-4 answers correct:**
  You are just starting to get to know Sprigatito.
- **5-6 answers correct:**
  It's certain that you're a big fan of Sprigatito.
- **7-8 answers correct:**
  Congratulations! Without a doubt, you're a Sprigatito expert!

ANSWERS ON PAGE 92

GUESS THE POKÉMON

Another round of stats and hints in the form of the Pokémon featured on this page, await you. Double-check the details and fill in the Pokémon names in the spaces provided.

1 **TYPE:** Grass/Normal
CATEGORY: Olive
IT MUST BE:

2 **TYPE:** Water
CATEGORY: Duckling
IT MUST BE:

3 **TYPE:** Fairy
CATEGORY: Puppy
IT MUST BE:

4 **TYPE:** Electric
CATEGORY: EleFrog
IT MUST BE:

5 **TYPE:** Fire/Psychic
CATEGORY: Fire Warrior
IT MUST BE:

6 **TYPE:** Dragon/Normal
CATEGORY: Mount
IT MUST BE:

ANSWERS ON PAGE 93

DARE TO DECODE

You succeeded at solving the first of these tests. Can you follow the correct twisted line to its corresponding empty space even faster this round? Time is of the essence!

THE POKÉMON PICTURED ON THIS PAGE ARE ALL

WHO'S THAT POKÉMON?

This round, Fuecoco needs help identifying its Fire-type Pokémon friends. Make sure you study each silhouette carefully before writing in your final decision.

1.

2.

3.

4.

5.

6.

ANSWERS ON PAGE 93

QUIZ QUEST

You can challenge yourself even further by setting a stopwatch. With or without the reference charts, how fast can you complete all four questions?

1 Which one of these Pokémon is NOT a dual type?

- A. Koraidon
- B. Miraidon
- C. Smoliv
- D. Bellibolt

2 Which one of these Pokémon can swim?

- A. Finneon
- B. Swablu
- C. Ralts
- D. Petilil

3 Which one of these Pokémon is NOT a Fire type?

- A. Amarouge
- B. Fuecoco
- C. Grafaiai
- D. Ceruledge

4 Which one of these Pokémon weighs more than 1,000 lbs.?

- A. Cetitan
- B. Great Tusk
- C. Dragonite
- D. Gyarados

ANSWERS ON PAGE 93

CLUED IN CLOSE-UP

Listen up! In this test, you need to trust your eyes. It takes a sharp eye to capture every detail and match Sprigatito's close-up image to its full image.

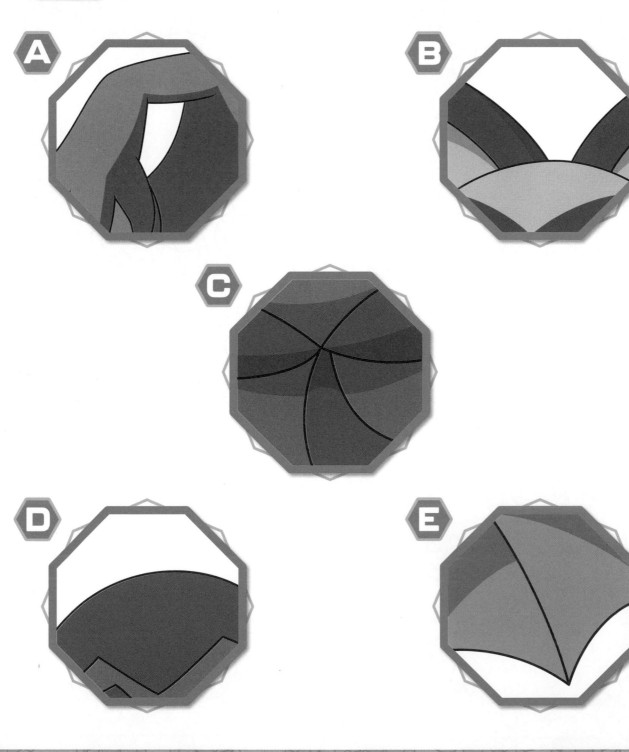

ANSWERS ON PAGE 93

STAND TALL AND MEASURE UP

Number these Pokémon from shortest to tallest from one to seven. Be careful, a few are very similar in height. Remember, if you need a little help, you can always refer to the height and weight charts at the back of this book.

ARMAROUGE

_____

LECHONK

_____

SPRIGATITO

_____

GREAT TUSK

_____

MIRAIDON

_____

GRAFAIAI

_____

PAWMI

_____

CROSSWORD CHALLENGE

Ten more Pokémon descriptions await you in this crossword puzzle. Don't forget, if you need a hint, look at the Pokémon pictured around the puzzle.

ANSWERS ON PAGE 93

3. This Terra Whale Pokémon wanders around snowy, icy areas. It protects its body with powerful muscles and a thick layer of fat under its skin.

5. This Ghost-type Pokémon startles people in the middle of the night. It gathers fear as its energy.

7. It protects itself from enemies by emitting oil from the fruit on its head. This oil is bitter and astringent enough to make someone flinch.

9. It carries food all day long. There are tales about lost people who were saved by the food that this Ice- and Flying-type Pokémon had.

10. It lives in groups in the treetops. If the Pig Monkey Pokémon loses sight of its group, it becomes infuriated by its loneliness.

1. This Bug- and Fighting-type Pokémon loves sweet nectar. To keep all the nectar to itself, it hurls rivals away with its prized horn.

2. It has underdeveloped electric sacs on its cheeks. These sacs can produce electricity only if this Mouse Pokémon rubs them furiously with the pads on its forepaws.

4. Now that the brain waves from the head and tail are synced up, the psychic power of this Pokémon is 10 times stronger than Girafarig's.

6. This cunning Dark- and Ice-type Pokémon hides under the cover of darkness, waiting to attack its prey.

8. This Pokémon lives in dark places untouched by sunlight. When it appears before humans, it hides itself under a cloth that resembles a Pikachu.

MIGHTY MAZE

Sprigatito and a Grass-type friend need to make it to the Grass-type symbol in the middle of the maze. It's up to you to lead two Pokémon to the center!

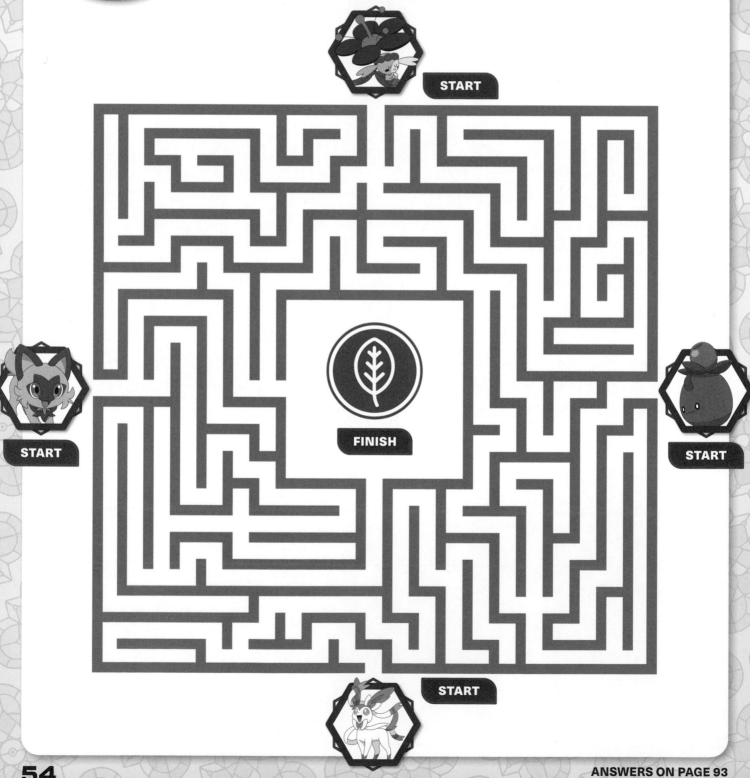

START

START

FINISH

START

START

ANSWERS ON PAGE 93

PATH OF THE FIRE-TYPE POKÉMON

It's Fuecoco's turn to make its way down a path through a maze of Pokémon. But it can only travel the path that Fire-type Pokémon have taken. Start at the top and help lead Fuecoco down to the finish line.

START

FINISH

DUAL-TYPE MATCH-UP

It's round two of the dual-type Pokémon challenge. All the details you will need to draw a line from the Pokémon's name to its corresponding types are in front of you. Choose wisely.

FARIGIRAF

GREAT TUSK

DRAGON/NORMAL

DRAGON/FLYING

NORMAL/PSYCHIC

GROUND/FIGHTING

GHOST/POISON

ELECTRIC/DRAGON

ELECTRIC/GHOST

WATER/PSYCHIC

HAUNTER

ROTOM

SLOWBRO

MIRAIDON

DRAGONITE

CYCLIZAR

ANSWERS ON PAGE 93

ARE YOU A FUECOCO EXPERT?

Are you an expert on Fuecoco? Could you prove it? Here's your chance! Think carefully before you answer the questions below. Your ranking depends upon it.

1 Height: _____

2 Weight: _____

3 Type: _____

4 It is a _____ Pokémon.

5 Fuecoco evolves into _____.

6 It lies on warm _____.

7 Fuecoco uses the heat absorbed by its square-shaped scales to create _____.

8 Its weaknesses are _____, _____, and _____.

- **1-2 answers correct:** You recognize who Fuecoco is, but you have much more to learn.
- **3-4 anwers correct:** You're just starting to get to know Fuecoco.
- **5-6 answers correct:** It's certain that you're a big fan of Fuecoco.
- **7-8 answers correct:** Congratulations! Without a doubt, you're a Fuecoco expert!

ANSWERS ON PAGE 93

PUZZLING OVER POKÉMON

Now it's Lechonk who is trying to sniff out a few key pieces to its puzzle. Don't forget, each piece only fits in a specific spot. Can you draw a line from each missing piece to its proper home?

ANSWERS ON PAGE 94

EYE ON EVOLUTION

True or false? You are a whiz at Evolution challenges. Here's your chance to prove that answer with this final true or false Evolution test. How will you do?

TRUE   FALSE

1 Dragonite is the final Evolution of Dragapult.

2 Eevee can evolve into 8 different forms.

3 Golduck evolves into Psyduck.

4 Igglybuff evolves into Jigglypuff before its final Evolution, Wigglytuff.

5 Gible's final Evolution is Garchomp.

6 Wiglett evolves into Diglett.

7 Shroodle evolves into Grafaiai.

8 Gastly evolves into Haunter before evolving into Gengar.

9 Chansey evolves into Hoppip.

10 Fletchling is a Tiny Robin Pokémon that's final Evolution is Talonflame.

ANSWERS ON PAGE 94

CLUED IN CLOSE-UP

Can you match Fidough's close-up image to its full image? You may think you know the answer right away. But double-check before you circle your final answer.

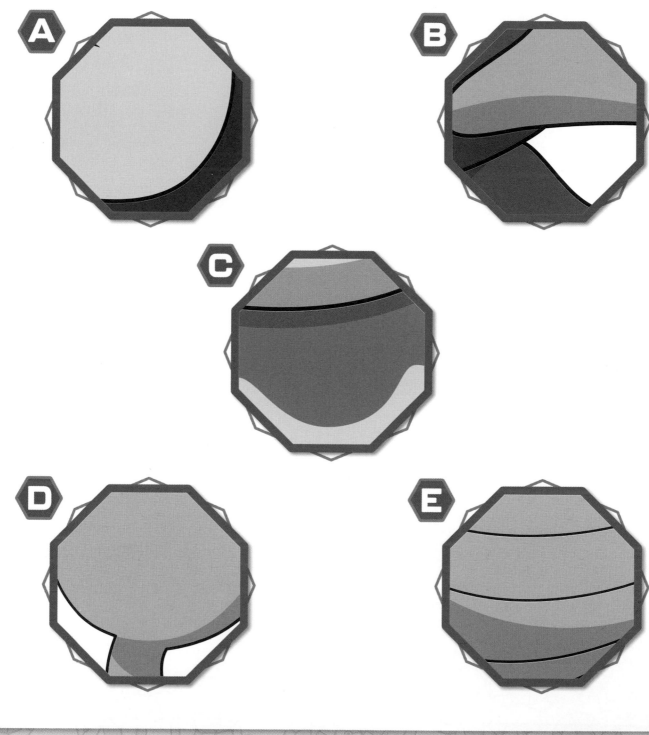

A

B

C

D

E

ANSWERS ON PAGE 94

SUDOKU
SKILL SET

To win this challenge, you must use four different Poké Balls to fill the grid below. We have started you off with four squares already filled in. Now you must fill the remaining squares. But keep in mind that you can only use a Poké Ball once in each column and row. You also cannot repeat a Poké Ball within the smaller 4x4 squares that are marked out in the grid.

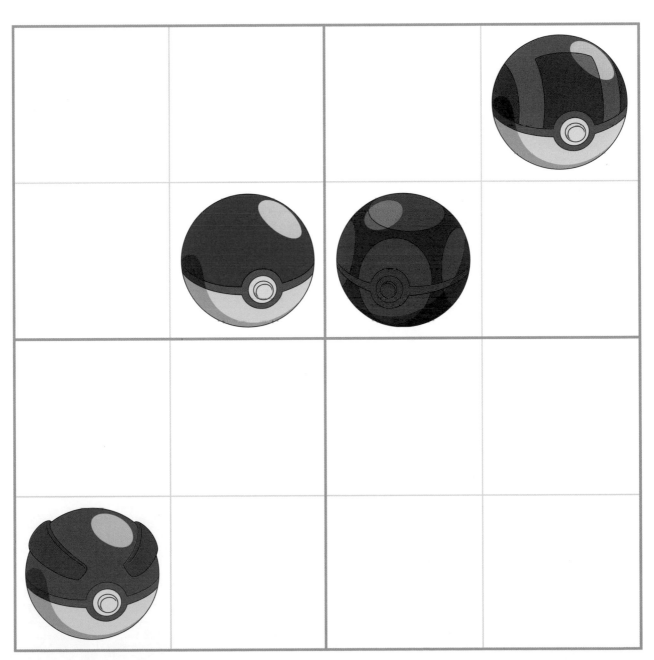

CROSSWORD CHALLENGE

Are your crossword puzzle skills improving? It's time to identify another ten Pokémon. Remember, you can use the Pokémon pictured to help you answer the descriptions to the crossword puzzle.

3. Once this Water- and Flying-type Pokémon appears, it goes on a rampage. It remains enraged until it demolishes everything around it.

6. It's said that no foe can remain invisible to this Fighting- and Steel Pokémon, since it can detect auras—even those of foes it could not otherwise see.

8. When this EleFrog Pokémon expands and contracts its wobbly body, the belly-button dynamo in its stomach produces a huge amount of electricity.

10. The fur on its body naturally repels water. This Aqua Mouse Pokémon can stay dry even when it plays in the water.

1. It's small and its electricity-generating organ is not fully developed, so this Electric- and Fairy-type Pokémon uses its tail to absorb electricity from people's home and charge itself.

2. This Pokémon's pincers, which contain steel, can crush any hard object they get ahold of into bits.

4. They communicate with one another using their auras. These Fighting-type Pokémon are able to run all though the night.

5. This Dark- and Ghost-type Pokémon dwells in the darkness of caves. It uses its sharp claws to dig up gems to nourish itself.

7. Apparently, this Dragon- and Normal-type Pokémon has been allowing people to ride on its back since ancient times. Depictions of this have been found in 10,000-year-old murals.

9. When they are young, female Pyroar will teach them how to hunt. Once they mature, they will leave the pride and set out on their own.

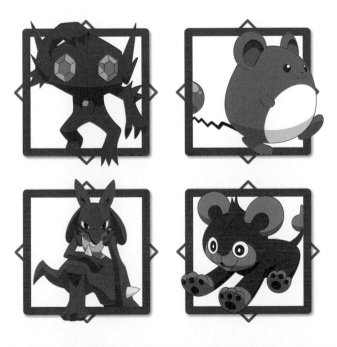

STAND TALL AND MEASURE UP

Number these Pokémon from shortest to tallest from one to seven. Be aware that a couple of them are almost the same height. Don't forget, if you get stuck, you can always refer to the height and weight charts at the back of this book.

GREAVARD

_____

KORAIDON

_____

SMOLIV

_____

CETITAN

_____

CERULEDGE

_____

BELLIBOLT

_____

FUECOCO

_____

ANSWERS ON PAGE 94

POKÉMON PATTERNS

For the final pattern maze, you need to follow four Pokémon type symbols from start to finish—Water, Fire, Grass, and Electric. Remember, in order to succeed at this test, you must always follow the same four Pokémon type symbol pattern exactly as shown below, over and over again as the pattern repeats, until you reach the end. You may only move horizontally and vertically.

KEY

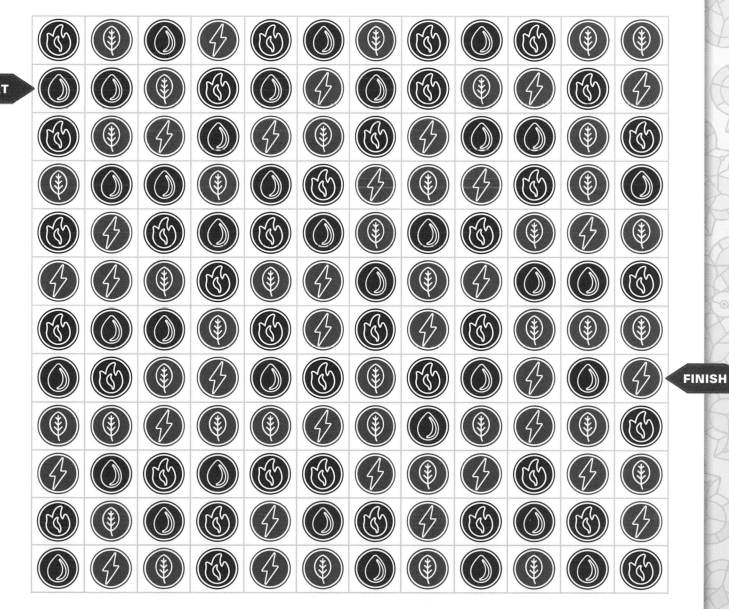

MIGHTY MAZE

Quaxly needs help searching out its Water-type friend all the while steering clear of any dual-type friends. Can you lead Quaxly to the correct exit?

START

FINISH

ANSWERS ON PAGE 94

DARE TO DECODE

Are you prepared for your last and final decoded message? It's a challenge for only the strongest Trainers.

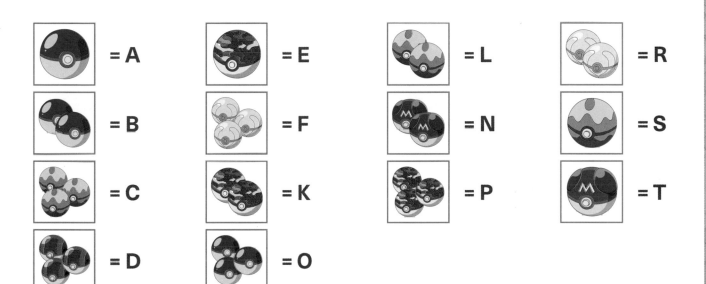

= A

= B

= C

= D

= E

= F

= K

= O

= L

= N

= P

= R

= S

= T

No worthy Trainer should leave home without their

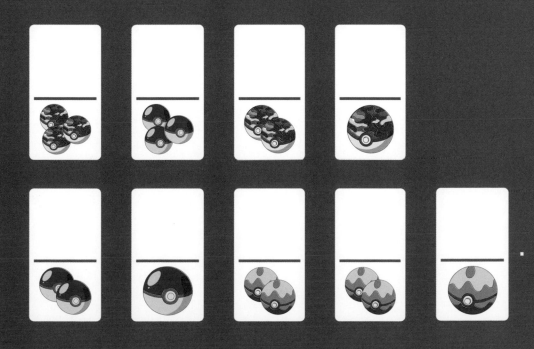

TIME TO TIP THE SCALES

Are you finding it tough to arrange the Pokémon in order from lightest to heaviest? Sometimes their heights and weights differ greatly in comparison. Remember, you can double-check your answers with the charts at the back of this book.

GREAVARD

BELLIBOLT

CYCLIZAR

QUAXLY

GREAT TUSK

WIGLETT

SMOLIV

ANSWER:

1 _____

2 _____

3 _____

4 _____

5 _____

6 _____

7 _____

ANSWERS ON PAGE 94

WORD SEARCH WONDER

Now, we will test your knowledge of even more detailed information on some of the newly discovered Paldea Pokémon. Can you name all 18 of the different categories that they belong to? Double-check your answers with the list below. Then, find and circle every one. Remember, you'll have to search across, down, and even diagonal!

```
P A R A D O X D U C K L I N G
T O X I C M O N K E Y G G L A
F I R E C R O C H G X A C O H
Q M F I R E B L A D E S A N V
U O O D J Y O D C V N H O G Y
F U U P H P V O O S Y A N P
S N A P S X E C L X R Z C E G
T T U B V E P E I R N Q X C R
E P A Z S W E D V C K I W K A
L R N L K N O V E P G K A U S
E F I R E W A R R I O R M H S
F M U D Q Y F X P Y Q V B C C
R X R K L S X M F J F L U U A
O A T E R R A W H A L E S A T
G H O S T D O G E W G G H U S
```

AMBUSH

DUCKLING

ELEFROG

FIRE BLADES

FIRE CROC

FIRE WARRIOR

GARDEN EEL

GHOST DOG

GRASS CAT

HOG

LONG NECK

MOUNT

MOUSE

OLIVE

PARADOX

PUPPY

TERRA WHALE

TOXIC MONKEY

SCRAMBLING TO UNSCRAMBLE

How fast can you help Pikachu unscramble the names of 5 more of its newly discovered friends from the Paldea region? Can you better your time by a whole minute from your last unscrambling round?

1 DUIHFGO

_____

2 AAFRGIIA

_____

3 DRNMIAIO

_____

4 OUCFCOE

_____

5 LVMOSI

_____

ANSWERS ON PAGE 95

QUIZ QUEST

The fourth and final quest awaits you. Can you better your time from the last round? Get ready. Get set. Go!

1 Which one of these Pokémon is shorter than 1'?

- ☐ A. Pawmi
- ☐ B. Fidough
- ☐ C. Azurill
- ☐ D. Lechonk

2 Which one of these Pokémon is NOT a Grass type?

- ☐ A. Cyclizar
- ☐ B. Smoliv
- ☐ C. Hoppip
- ☐ D. Sprigatito

3 Which one of these Pokémon is NOT a Paldea first partner Pokémon?

- ☐ A. Quaxly
- ☐ B. Fidough
- ☐ C. Sprigatito
- ☐ D. Fuecoco

4 Which one of these Pokémon does NOT evolve?

- ☐ A. Klawf
- ☐ B. Wiglett
- ☐ C. Girafarig
- ☐ D. Pikachu

ANSWERS ON PAGE 95

DUAL-TYPE MATCH-UP

They say the third time's the charm. Is it for you in this dual-type match-up challenge? Let's see how you do. Draw a line from each Pokémon to its dual-type name.

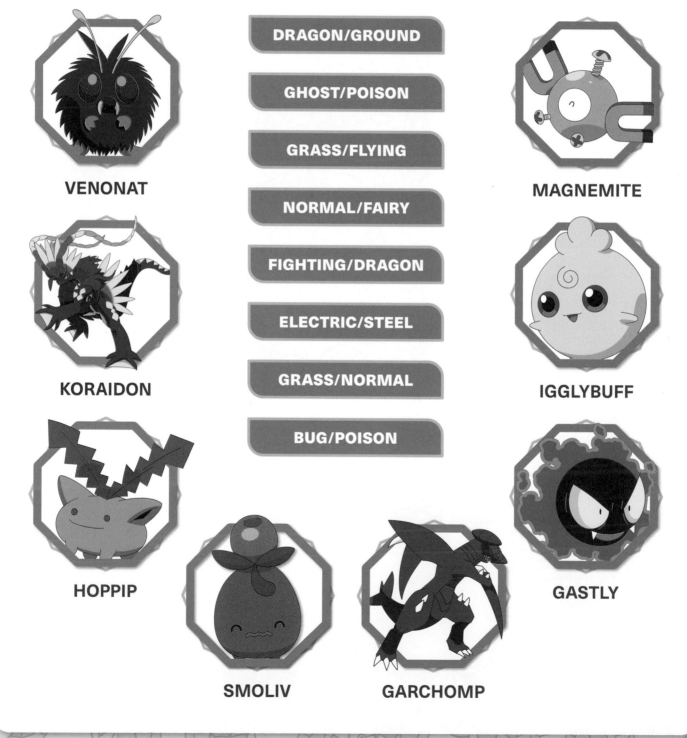

VENONAT

KORAIDON

HOPPIP

DRAGON/GROUND

GHOST/POISON

GRASS/FLYING

NORMAL/FAIRY

FIGHTING/DRAGON

ELECTRIC/STEEL

GRASS/NORMAL

BUG/POISON

MAGNEMITE

IGGLYBUFF

GASTLY

SMOLIV

GARCHOMP

ANSWERS ON PAGE 95

CLUED IN CLOSE-UP

Can you match Fuecoco's close-up image to its full image? Only the most tail-ented Trainer will be able to weed out the competition and circle the correct answer.

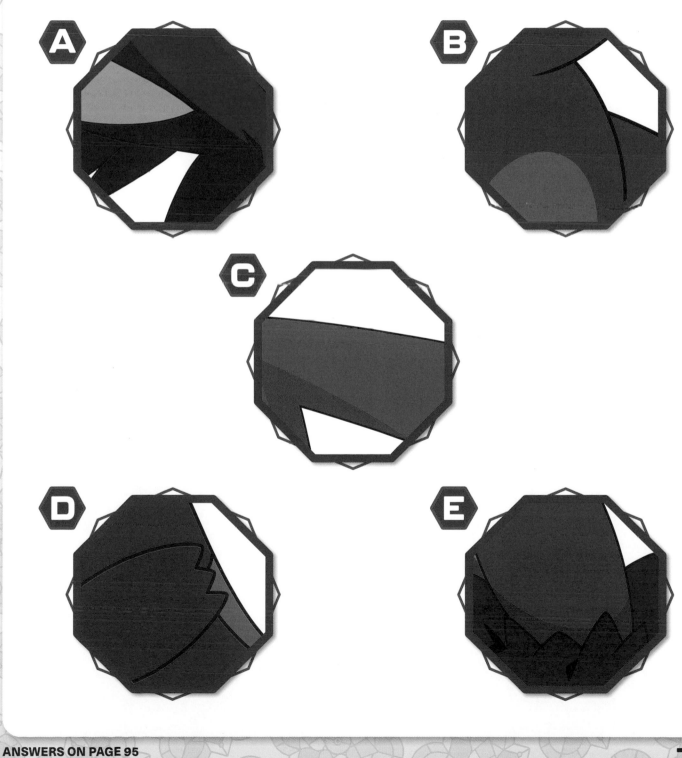

PATH OF THE ELECTRIC-TYPE POKÉMON

In this final test, Pikachu needs help making its way down a path through a maze of Pokémon. But remember, it can't travel outside the path of its type—the path that Electric-type Pokémon have taken. Start at the top and lead Pikachu down to the finish line.

START

FINISH

ANSWERS ON PAGE 95

ARE YOU A PIKACHU EXPERT?

Are you an expert on Pikachu? Could you prove it? Here's your chance! Think carefully before you answer the questions below. Your ranking depends upon it.

1 Height: _____

2 Weight: _____

3 Type: _____

4 It is a _____ Pokémon.

5 Pikachu evolves into _____.

6 When it is angered, it immediately discharges the _____ stored in the pouches in its cheeks.

7 Pikachu's weakness is _____.

8 The tips of Pikachu's ears are the color _____.

- **1-2 answers correct:**
  You recognize who Pikachu is, but you have much more to learn.

- **3-4 answers correct:**
  You're just starting to get to know Pikachu.

- **5-6 answers correct:**
  It's certain that you're a big fan of Pikachu.

- **7-8 answers correct:**
  Congratulations! Without a doubt, you are a Pikachu expert!

ANSWERS ON PAGE 95

MIGHTY MAZE

The Paldea first partner Pokémon are at the very center of this maze. But each one needs to find its way out to its unique exit. Can you guess what that might be? Look for its specific type symbol to lead the way: Sprigatito to Grass type, Fuecoco to Fire type, and Quaxly to Water type.

FINISH

FINISH

START

FINISH

ANSWERS ON PAGE 95

GUESS THE POKÉMON

It's time for one final round of Pokédex stats. How will you do? If you get stuck and need a hint, remember to take a closer look at the Pokémon pictured on this page.

1
TYPE: Grass
CATEGORY: Grass Cat
IT MUST BE:

2
TYPE: Rock
CATEGORY: Ambush
IT MUST BE:

3
TYPE: Ghost
CATEGORY: Ghost Dog
IT MUST BE:

4
TYPE: Normal
CATEGORY: Hog
IT MUST BE:

5
TYPE: Electric
CATEGORY: Mouse
IT MUST BE:

6
TYPE: Poison/Normal
CATEGORY: Toxic Monkey
IT MUST BE:

PUZZLING OVER POKÉMON

It's time to help Fuecoco find a few key pieces to its puzzle. Remember, each piece only fits in a specific spot. Draw a line from each missing piece to its proper home and complete the puzzle!

ANSWERS ON PAGE 95

SUDOKU SKILL SET

To win this challenge, you must use four different berries to fill the grid below. We have started you off with four squares already filled in. Now you must fill the remaining squares. But keep in mind that you can only use a berry once in each column and row. You also cannot repeat a berry within the smaller 4x4 squares that are marked out in the grid.

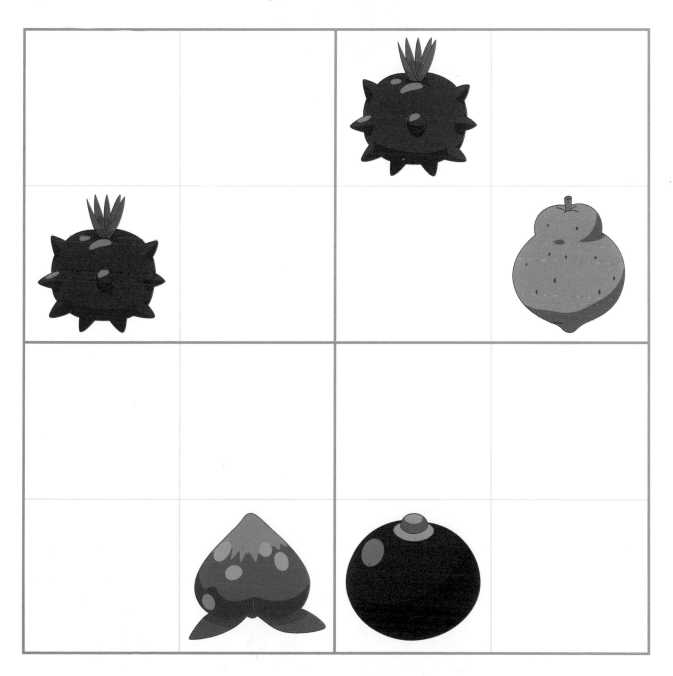

CROSSWORD CHALLENGE

This is your last chance to test your crossword puzzle skills. Identify these ten Pokémon described in the clues. Your hints—the Pokémon surrounding the puzzle—are there if you need them. Good luck!

ANSWERS ON PAGE 96

4. This EleSquirrel Pokémon with electric cheek pouches shoots charges from its tail.

7. This Fire Warrior Pokémon evolved through the use of a set of armor that belonged to a distinguished warrior. This Pokémon is incredibly loyal.

8. It can't see, so its first approach to examining things is to bite them. You will be covered in wounds until it warms up to you.

9. This Psychic-type Pokémon will die if it stops bouncing. The pearl on its head amplifies its psychic powers.

10. This Grass-type Pokémon spreads a sweet scent that makes others feel invigorated. This same scent is popular for antiperspirants.

1. This Fighting-type Pokémon battles by throwing hard berries. It won't obey a Trainer who throws Poké Balls without skill.

2. This Pokémon is very friendly when it's young. Its disposition becomes vicious once it matures, but it never forgets the kindness of its master.

3. When exposed to the moon's aura, the rings on its body glow faintly and it gains a mysterious power.

5. It flies around on its wings, which have grown in at last. In its happiness, it gushes hot flames, burning up everything it passes over.

6. The fiery blades on this Fire- and Ghost-type Pokémon's arms burn fiercely with the lingering resentment of a sword wielder who fell before accomplishing their goal.

CONNECT THE POKÉ BALL

With a steady hand, count to 25 and connect the dots to reveal the hidden Poké Ball within.

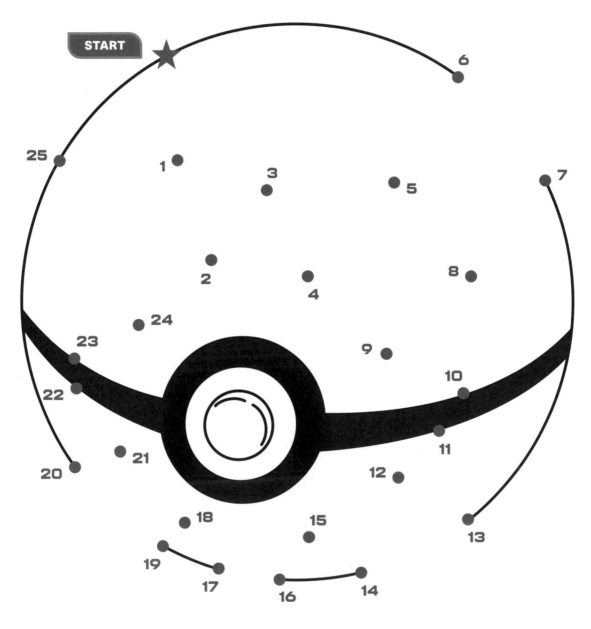

START

6

25   1   3   5   7

2   8

4

24

23   9

22   10

21   11

20   12

18   15

19   17   16   14   13

ANSWERS ON PAGE 96

TIME TO TIP THE SCALES

Tip the scales one last time and arrange these Pokémon in order from lightest to heaviest. The height and weight charts at the back of this book are there to refer to if need be.

CERULEDGE

SPRIGATITO

KORAIDON

FARIGIRAF

FIDOUGH

LECHONK

ARMAROUGE

ANSWER:

1 _____

2 _____

3 _____

4 _____

5 _____

6 _____

7 _____

ANSWERS ON PAGE 96

SCRAMBLING TO UNSCRAMBLE

Do you think you can score your personal best time in your final unscrambling round? Let's see just how fast you can help Pikachu unscramble the names of these last five newly discovered friends from the Paldea region. Ready, set, GO!

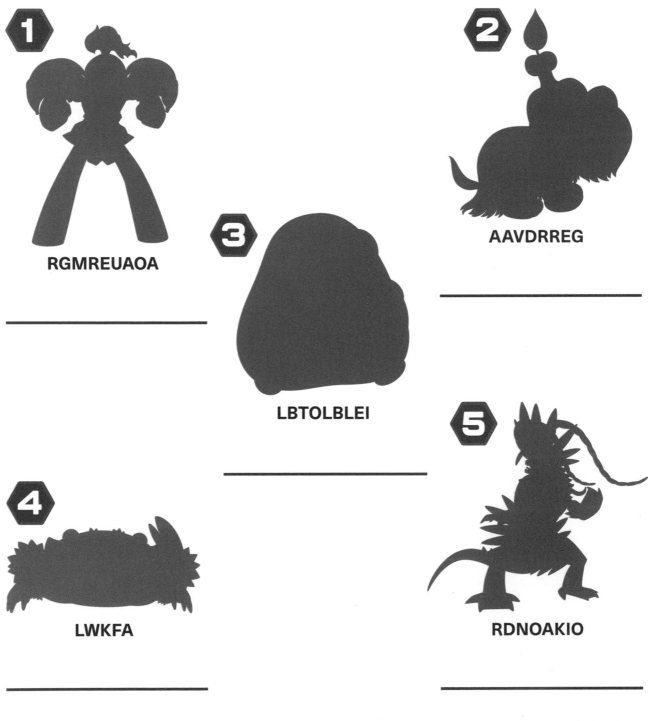

1 RGMREUAOA

_____

2 AAVDRREG

_____

3 LBTOLBLEI

_____

4 LWKFA

_____

5 RDNOAKIO

_____

ANSWERS ON PAGE 96

POKÉMON DREAM TEAM

If you could create your Pokémon dream team to travel with you on your adventures, which six newly discovered Pokémon from Paldea would you choose and why? Your choices can be based on anything that matters most to you—type, size, cuteness, etc.

1 I would choose _____

because _____.

2 I would choose _____

because _____.

3 I would choose _____

because _____.

4 I would choose _____

because _____.

5 I would choose _____

because _____.

6 I would choose _____

because _____.

PALDEA SEARCH AND FIND

Get ready for one last countdown! It's time to go back through the book (pages 6-85) and count up the following artwork that appears within the puzzles and activities—including some of the newly discovered Paldea region Pokémon!

HOW MANY TIMES DID YOU SEE THE EXACT ARTWORK. . .?

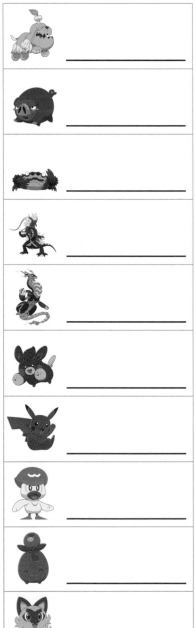

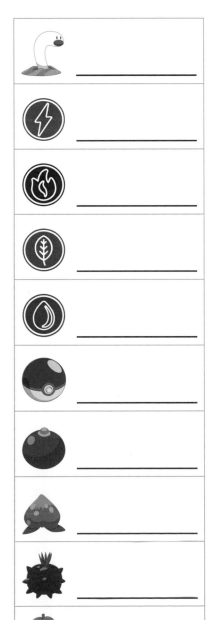

ANSWERS ON PAGE 96

HOW MANY TIMES DID YOU SEE THE FOLLOWING TEXT. . .?

ARMAROUGE _____

BELLIBOLT _____

CERULEDGE _____

CETITAN _____

CYCLIZAR _____

FARIGIRAF _____

FIDOUGH _____

FUECOCO _____

GRAFAIAI _____

GREAT TUSK _____

GREAVARD _____

KLAWF _____

KORAIDON _____

LECHONK _____

MIRAIDON _____

PAWMI _____

PIKACHU _____

QUAXLY _____

SLOWBRO _____

SMOLIV _____

SPRIGATITO _____

WIGLETT _____

BUG _____

DARK _____

DRAGON _____

ELECTRIC _____

FAIRY _____

FIGHTING _____

FIRE _____

FLYING _____

GHOST _____

GRASS _____

GROUND _____

ICE _____

NORMAL _____

POISON _____

PSYCHIC _____

ROCK _____

STEEL _____

WATER _____

PALDEA _____

POKÉMON _____

POKÉ BALL _____

CONGRATS CHAMPION!

You've completed your challenge and proven
your Paldea region knowledge is strong.
Date and sign your champion certificate. You earned it!

NAME: _____

DATE STARTED: _____

DATE COMPLETED: _____

ANSWER KEY

SPRIGATITO, FUECOCO, AND QUAXLY ARE FIRST PARTNER PALDEA POKÉMON.

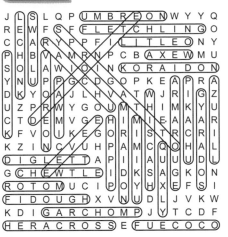

C

1. CERULEDGE

2. FARIGIRAF

3. PAWMI

4. QUAXLY

5. WIGLETT

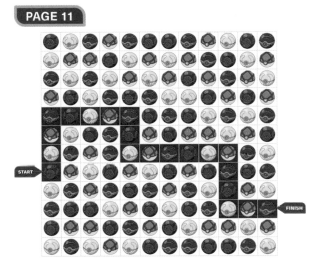

1. C) LECHONK
2. D) SMOLIV
3. C) SPRIGATITO
4. B) KORAIDON

1. TRUE
2. TRUE
3. FALSE
4. FALSE
5. TRUE
6. FALSE
7. FALSE
8. TRUE
9. FALSE
10. TRUE

1. MIRAIDON
2. CETITAN
3. KORAIDON
4. FUECOCO
5. CERULEDGE
6. GREAT TUSK

1. FIDOUGH 1'
2. QUAXLY 1' 8"
3. WIGLETT 3' 11"
4. KLAWF 4' 3"
5. CYCLIZAR 5' 3"
6. FARIGRAF 10' 6"

PAGE 17

ARMAROUGE FIRE/PSYCHIC
CERULEDGE FIRE/GHOST
FLETCHLING NORMAL/FLYING
GRAFAIAI POISON/NORMAL
GYARADOS WATER/FLYING
KROKOROK GROUND/DARK
LARVITAR ROCK/GROUND
SWABLU NORMAL/FLYING

PAGE 18

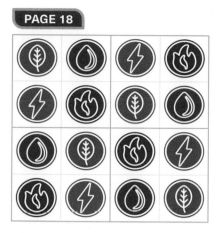

PAGE 19

THIS NORMAL-TYPE POKÉMON, LECHONK, SEARCHES FOR FOOD ALL DAY WITH ITS KEEN SENSE OF SMELL.

PAGE 20

PAGE 21

PAGE 22

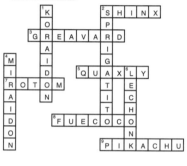

PAGE 24

1. BOUNSWEET   2. LEAFEON   3. HOPPIP

4. STEENEE   5. LURANTIS   6. CACNEA

PAGE 25

1. 1' 8"   5. QUAXWELL
2. 13.4 LBS.   6. HAT
3. WATER   7. WATER AND GRIME
4. DUCKLING   8. GRASS AND ELECTRIC

PAGE 26

NOT EVERY POKÉMON EVOLVES.

SPRIGATITO   LECHONK   FUECOCO   QUAXLY

GRAFAIAI   ARMAROUGE   CYCLIZAR   CETITAN

H	T	W	L	W	F	I	G	H	T	I	N	G	Y	N
B	M	A	J	F	M	M	H	W	V	A	D	T	M	O
W	N	U	X	B	F	T	O	O	E	D	R	M	Y	R
S	Z	C	K	R	G	Q	S	R	N	H	A	K	P	M
T	D	G	U	S	O	R	T	F	S	H	G	S	O	A
Y	U	U	S	H	Q	C	A	C	M	K	O	H	B	L
T	I	F	T	G	T	U	K	S	C	A	N	D	W	C
H	L	R	I	E	A	O	B	Q	S	B	C	I	G	H
A	J	E	L	E	C	T	R	I	C	I	U	U	V	P
M	G	B	B	V	T	T	Q	J	Y	C	R	G	H	O
L	W	R	P	S	Y	C	H	I	C	E	Z	V	D	I
Q	K	M	T	S	C	Q	C	S	T	C	S	S	O	S
P	V	E	D	A	R	K	F	A	I	R	Y	R	V	O
N	W	P	F	I	R	E	W	G	R	O	U	N	D	N
F	L	Y	I	N	G	S	T	E	E	L	G	I	Q	Q

E

1. B) GREAVARD
2. D) GYARADOS
3. D) CERULEDGE
4. A) CETITAN

1. PAWMI 5.5 LBS.
2. FUECOCO 21.6 LBS.
3. GRAFAIAI 60 LBS.
4. KLAWF 174.2 LBS.
5. MIRAIDON 529.1 LBS.
6. CETITAN 1543.2 LBS.

START

FINISH   FINISH   FINISH

1. 1' 8"
2. 22.5 LBS.
3. NORMAL
4. HOG
5. OINKOLOGNE
6. SENSE OF SMELL
7. FOOD
8. PINK

START

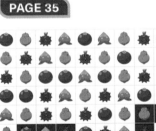

FINISH

1. CETITAN   2. CYCLIZAR   3. GREAT TUSK   4. LECHONK   5. SPRIGATITO

1. PSYDUCK

2. MAGIKARP

3. GASTRODON

4. MARILL

5. CHEWTLE

6. VAPOREON

PAGE 38

PAGE 39

PAGE 40

1. BELLIBOLT, CETITAN, FIDOUGH, FUECOCO, GREAVARD, KLAWF, LECHONK, PAWMI, QUAXLY, SPRIGATITO, WIGLETT
2. CYCLIZAR, GREAT TUSK, KLAWF, KORAIDON, MIRAIDON
3. FARIGIRAF, FIDOUGH, GREAT TUSK, GREAVARD, LECHONK, PAWMI, SPRIGATITO
4. MIRAIDON, KORAIDON
5. FIDOUGH, FUECOCO, LECHONK, PAWMI, QUAXLY, SMOLIV, SPRIGATITO
6. ARMAROUGE, CERULEDGE, CYCLIZAR, FARIGIRAF, GRAFAIAI, GREAT TUSK, KORAIDON, MIRAIDON, SMOLIV
7. ARMAROUGE, BELLIBOLT, CERULEDGE, CETITAN, CYCLIZAR, FARIGIRAF, GREAT TUSK, KLAWF, KORAIDON, MIRAIDON
8. CETITAN, CYCLIZAR, FARIGIRAF, FIDOUGH, FUECOCO, GRAFAIAI, GREAT TUSK, GREAVARD, KORAIDON, LECHONK, MIRAIDON, PAWMI, QUAXLY, SPRIGATITO

PAGE 41

1. FALSE
2. FALSE
3. TRUE
4. FALSE
5. TRUE
6. FALSE
7. FALSE
8. TRUE
9. TRUE
10. TRUE

PAGE 42

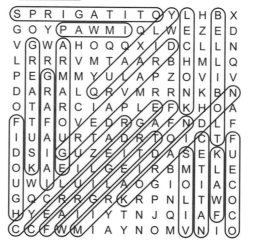

PAGE 44

PAGE 45

1. 1' 4"
2. 9 LBS.
3. GRASS
4. GRASS CAT
5. FLORAGATO
6. WASHES ITS FACE
7. PINK
8. PLANTS

PAGE 46

1. SMOLIV
2. QUAXLY
3. FIDOUGH
4. BELLIBOLT
5. ARMAROUGE
6. CYCLIZAR

PAGE 47

THE POKÉMON PICTURED ON THIS PAGE ARE ALL DUAL TYPE.

PAGE 48

1. FLAREON   2. TORKOAL   3. ARCANINE

4. GROWLITHE   5. ARMAROUGE   6. CERULEDGE

PAGE 49

1. D) BELLIBOLT
2. A) FINNEON
3. C) GRAFAIAI
4. A) CETITAN

PAGE 50

PAGE 51

1. PAWMI — 1'
2. SPRIGATITO — 1' 4"
3. LECHONK — 1' 8"
4. GRAFAIAI — 2' 4"
5. ARMAROUGE — 4' 11"
6. GREAT TUSK — 7' 3"
7. MIRAIDON — 11' 6"

PAGE 52

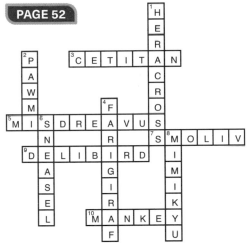

Across:
3. CETITAN
5. MISDREAVUS
7. SMOLIV
9. DELIBIRD
10. MANKEY

Down:
1. HERACROSS
2. PAWMI
4. FRIGIBAX
5. MINK (MIMIKYU)
8. SIMISEAR

PAGE 54

START / FINISH / START / START / START

PAGE 55

START ... FINISH

PAGE 56

CYCLIZAR — DRAGON/NORMAL
DRAGONITE — DRAGON/FLYING
FARIGIRAF — NORMAL/PSYCHIC
GREAT TUSK — GROUND/FIGHTING
HAUNTER — GHOST/POISON
MIRAIDON — ELECTRIC/DRAGON
ROTOM — ELECTRIC/GHOST
SLOWBRO — WATER/PSYCHIC

PAGE 57

1. 1' 4"
2. 21.6 LBS.
3. FIRE
4. FIRE CROC
5. CROCALOR
6. ROCKS
7. FIRE ENERGY
8. WATER, GROUND, AND ROCK

PAGE 58

PAGE 59

1. FALSE
2. TRUE
3. FALSE
4. TRUE
5. TRUE
6. FALSE
7. TRUE
8. TRUE
9. FALSE
10. TRUE

PAGE 60

PAGE 61

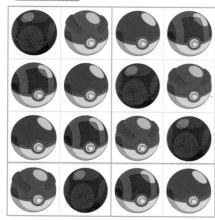

PAGE 62

PAGE 64

1. SMOLIV — 1'
2. FUECOCO — 1' 4"
3. GREAVARD — 2'
4. BELLIBOLT — 3' 11"
5. CERULEDGE — 5' 3"
6. KORAIDON — 8' 2"
7. CETITAN — 14'

PAGE 65

PAGE 66

PAGE 67

NO WORTHY
TRAINER SHOULD
LEAVE HOME
WITHOUT THEIR
POKÉ BALLS.

PAGE 68

1. WIGLETT — 4 LBS.
2. QUAXLY — 13.4 LBS.
3. SMOLIV — 14.3 LBS.
4. GREAVARD — 77.2 LBS.
5. CYCLIZAR — 138.9 LBS.
6. BELLIBOLT — 249.1 LBS.
7. GREAT TUSK — 705.5 LBS.

```
P A R A D O X D U C K L I N G
T O X I C M O N K E Y G G L A H
F I R E C R O C H G X A C O N V
Q M F I R E B L A D E S A N
U O O D J Y O D C V N H O G N E
F U U U P H P V O O S Y A N C G
S N A P S X E C L X R Z C E K R
T T U B V E P E I R N Q X U A
E P A Z S W E D V C K I W B S
L R N L K N O V E P G K H U C A
E F I R E W A R R I O R M B A T
F M U D Q Y F X P Y Q V B C U A
R X R K L S X M F J F L H U A U
Q A T E R R A W H A L E S A U S
G H O S T D O G E W G G H U S
```

1. FIDOUGH 2. GRAFAIAI

3. MIRAIDON 4. FUECOCO 5. SMOLIV

1. C) AZURILL
2. A) CYCLIZAR
3. B) FIDOUGH
4. A) KLAWF

GARCHOMP	DRAGON/GROUND
GASTLY	GHOST/POISON
HOPPIP	GRASS/FLYING
IGGLYBUFF	NORMAL/FAIRY
KORAIDON	FIGHTING/DRAGON
MAGNEMITE	ELECTRIC/STEEL
SMOLIV	GRASS/NORMAL
VENONAT	BUG/POISON

D

1. 1' 4"
2. 13.2 LBS.
3. ELECTRIC
4. MOUSE
5. RAICHU
6. ENERGY
7. GROUND
8. BLACK

1. SPRIGATITO
2. KLAWF
3. GREAVARD
4. LECHONK
5. PAWMI
6. GRAFAIAI

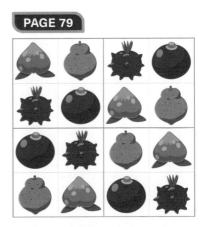

Crossword answers:
- 1. PASS
- 2. ROCKRUFF
- 4. PACHIRISU
- 3. UMBREON
- 5. SMALLMEACE
- 6. CERULLCDG
- 7. ARMAROUGE
- 8. DEINO
- 9. SPOINK
- 10. STEENEE

START

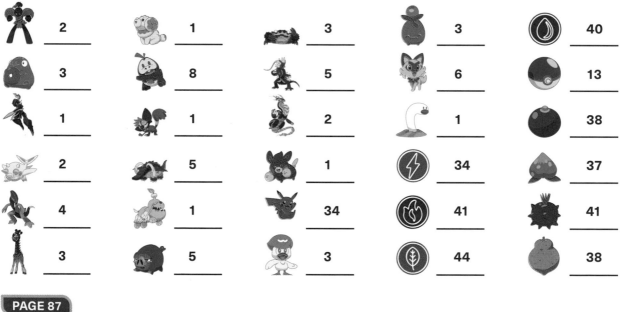

1. SPRIGATITO   9 LBS.
2. LECHONK   22.5 LBS.
3. FIDOUGH   24 LBS.
4. CERULEDGE   136.7 LBS.
5. ARMAROUGE   187.4 LBS.
6. FARIGIRAF   352.7 LBS.
7. KORAIDON   668 LBS.

1. ARMAROUGE   2. GREAVARD   3. BELLIBOLT   4. KLAWF   5. KORAIDON

2		1		3		3		40
3		8		5		6		13
1		1		2		1		38
2		5		1		34		37
4		1		34		41		41
3		5		3		44		38

ARMAROUGE: 8
BELLIBOLT: 4
CERULEDGE: 7
CETITAN: 7
CYCLIZAR: 9
FARIGIRAF: 6
FIDOUGH: 8
FUECOCO: 24
GRAFAIAI: 7
GREAT TUSK: 7
GREAVARD: 5

KLAWF: 4
KORAIDON: 7
LECHONK: 16
MIRAIDON: 7
PAWMI: 6
PIKACHU: 24
QUAXLY: 24
SLOWBRO: 1
SMOLIV: 6
SPRIGATITO: 20
WIGLETT: 5

BUG: 3
DARK: 5
DRAGON: 13
ELECTRIC: 18
FAIRY: 6
FIGHTING: 11
FIRE: 24
FLYING: 9
GHOST: 12
GRASS: 18
GROUND: 8

ICE: 4
NORMAL: 14
POISON: 6
PSYCHIC: 9
ROCK: 3
STEEL: 5
WATER: 16
PALDEA: 16
POKÉMON: 152
POKÉ BALL: 9

Pikachu's yellow tail will catch your attention and take you to the correct page in a flash of lightning!

PIKACHU
(PEE-ka-choo)

When Pikachu is angered, it immediately discharges the energy stored in the pouches in its cheeks.

ELECTRIC TYPE

HEIGHT: 1' 4"

WEIGHT: 13.2 LBS.

FOLDING INSTRUCTIONS

1

The dotted lines on the template are fold lines to help guide you.

Start with the template with Pikachu facing you at the bottom.

2

Turn over to the back side and fold in half, matching the two corners together.

3

Fold the top corner of just the first layer down to where the middle fold is.

4

Fold both bottom corners in to reach the top corner.

5

Fold the two top corners of the front layer down to meet the bottom corner. Crease and then unfold.

6

Tuck in the two corners into the bottom triangle in the middle layer.

Flip over, and your bookmark is ready to use!

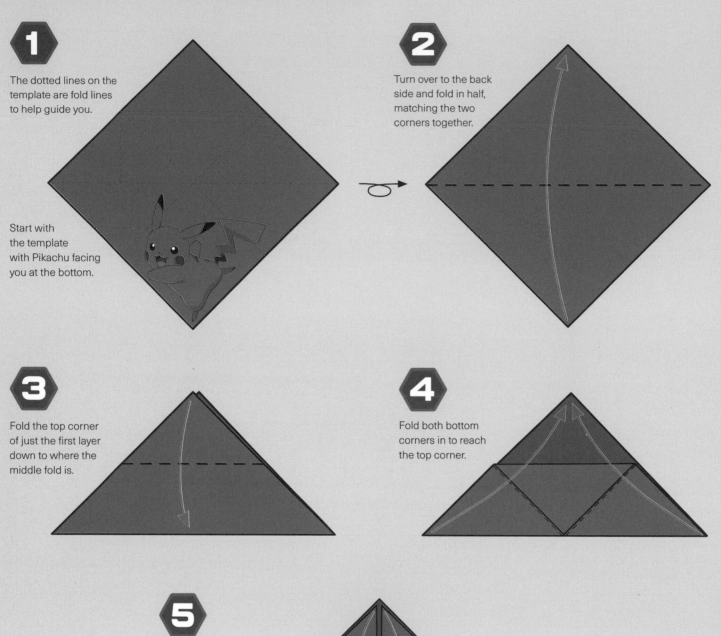

BOOKMARK TEMPLATE

Cut this template page out. Then cut along the outer square edge of the template below as highlighted in blue to the right. Carefully cut along the top of Pikachu's ear and the top of its tail just up to the dotted fold lines.

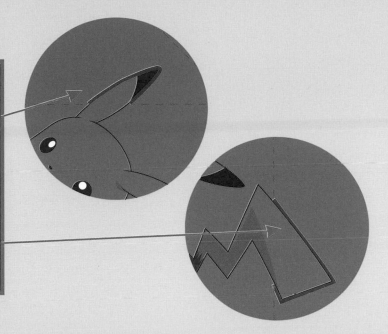

Sprigatito's green perked-up ears will catch the sound of you flipping through the pages and quickly lead you to where you left off in your reading.

SPRIGATITO
(SPRIG-uh-TEE-toh)

Sprigatito's fluffy fur is similar in composition to plants. This Pokémon frequently washes its face to keep it from drying out.

GRASS TYPE

HEIGHT: 1' 4"

WEIGHT: 9 LBS.

FOLDING INSTRUCTIONS

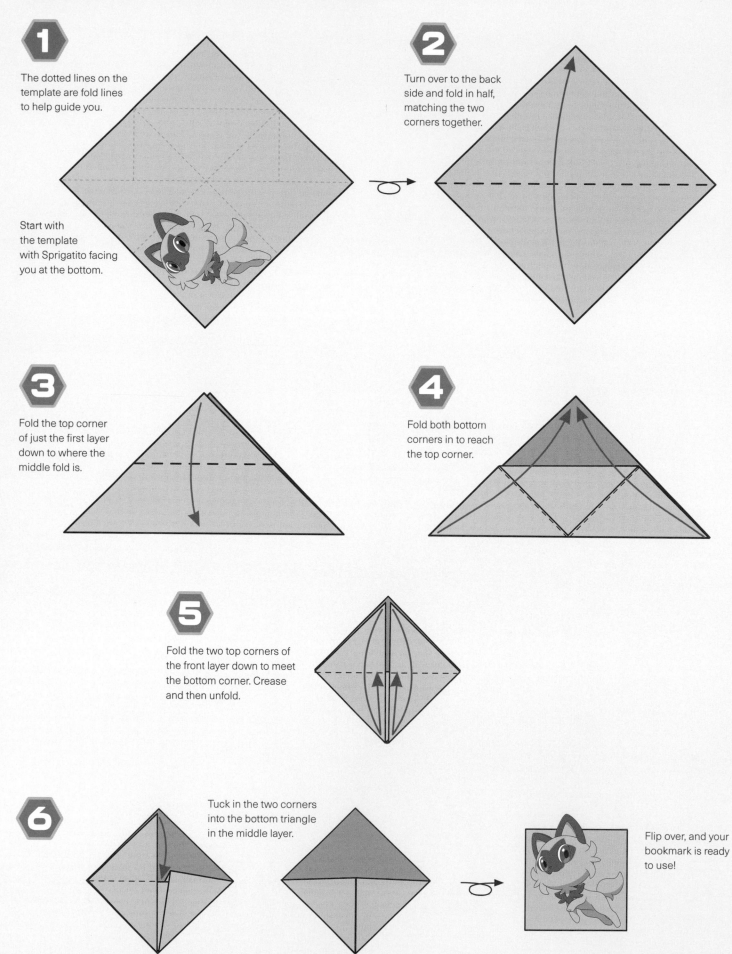

1

The dotted lines on the template are fold lines to help guide you.

Start with the template with Sprigatito facing you at the bottom.

2

Turn over to the back side and fold in half, matching the two corners together.

3

Fold the top corner of just the first layer down to where the middle fold is.

4

Fold both bottom corners in to reach the top corner.

5

Fold the two top corners of the front layer down to meet the bottom corner. Crease and then unfold.

6

Tuck in the two corners into the bottom triangle in the middle layer.

Flip over, and your bookmark is ready to use!

BOOKMARK TEMPLATE

Cut this template page out. Then cut along the outer square edge of the template below as highlighted in blue to the right. Carefully cut along the top of Sprigatito's ear just up to the dotted fold lines.

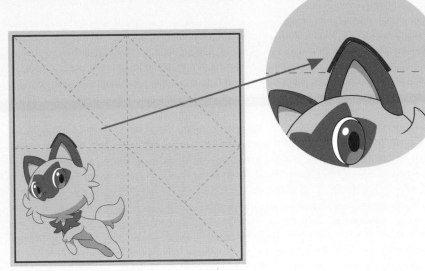

Fuecoco's yellow tufts on the top of its head will fire up your imagination and lead you right back to where you left off reading.

FUECOCO
(fwey-KO-ko)

Fuecoco lies on warm rocks and uses the heat absorbed by its square-shaped scales to create fire energy.

FIRE TYPE

HEIGHT: 1' 4"

WEIGHT: 21.6 LBS.

FOLDING INSTRUCTIONS

1

The dotted lines on the template are fold lines to help guide you.

Start with the template with Fuecoco facing you at the bottom.

2

Turn over to the back side and fold in half, matching the two corners together.

3

Fold the top corner of just the first layer down to where the middle fold is.

4

Fold both bottom corners in to reach the top corner.

5

Fold the two top corners of the front layer down to meet the bottom corner. Crease and then unfold.

6

Tuck in the two corners into the bottom triangle in the middle layer.

Flip over, and your bookmark is ready to use!

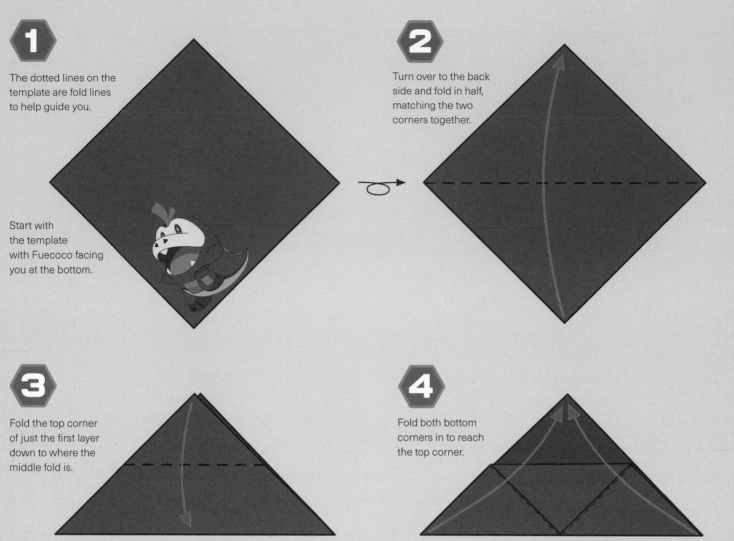
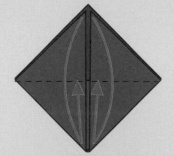
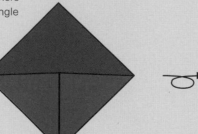

BOOKMARK TEMPLATE

Cut this template page out. Then cut along the outer square edge of the template below as highlighted in blue to the right. Carefully cut along the top of Fuecoco's yellow tuft just up to the dotted fold lines.

Quaxly's signature blue hat peaking above the page will stop you in your tracks and remind you where you last stopped reading.

QUAXLY
(KWACKS-lee)

Quaxly migrated to Paldea from distant lands long ago. The gel secreted by Its feathers repels water and grime.

WATER TYPE

HEIGHT: 1' 8"

WEIGHT: 13.4 LBS.

FOLDING INSTRUCTIONS

1

The dotted lines on the template are fold lines to help guide you.

Start with the template with Quaxly facing you at the bottom.

2

Turn over to the back side and fold in half, matching the two corners together.

3

Fold the top corner of just the first layer down to where the middle fold is.

4

Fold both bottom corners in to reach the top corner.

5

Fold the two top corners of the front layer down to meet the bottom corner. Crease and then unfold.

6

Tuck in the two corners into the bottom triangle in the middle layer.

Flip over, and your bookmark is ready to use!

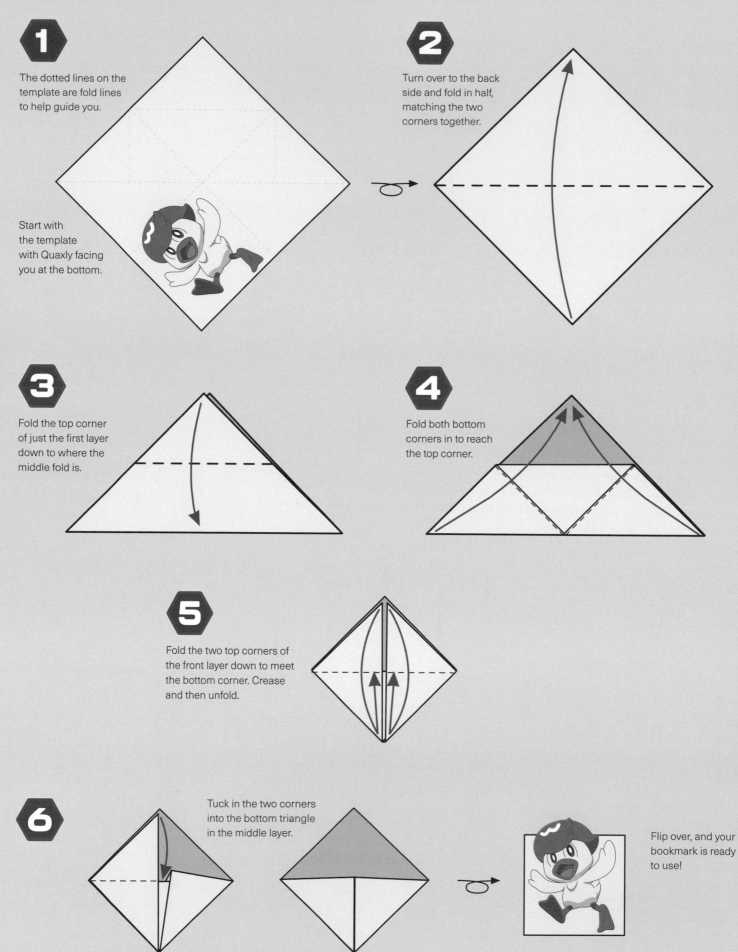

BOOKMARK TEMPLATE

Cut this template page out. Then cut along the outer square edge of the template below as highlighted in blue to the right. Carefully cut along the top of Quaxly's hat on top of its head just up to the dotted fold lines.